Perspect;ve

Perspect;ve

By

Kristofer D. West

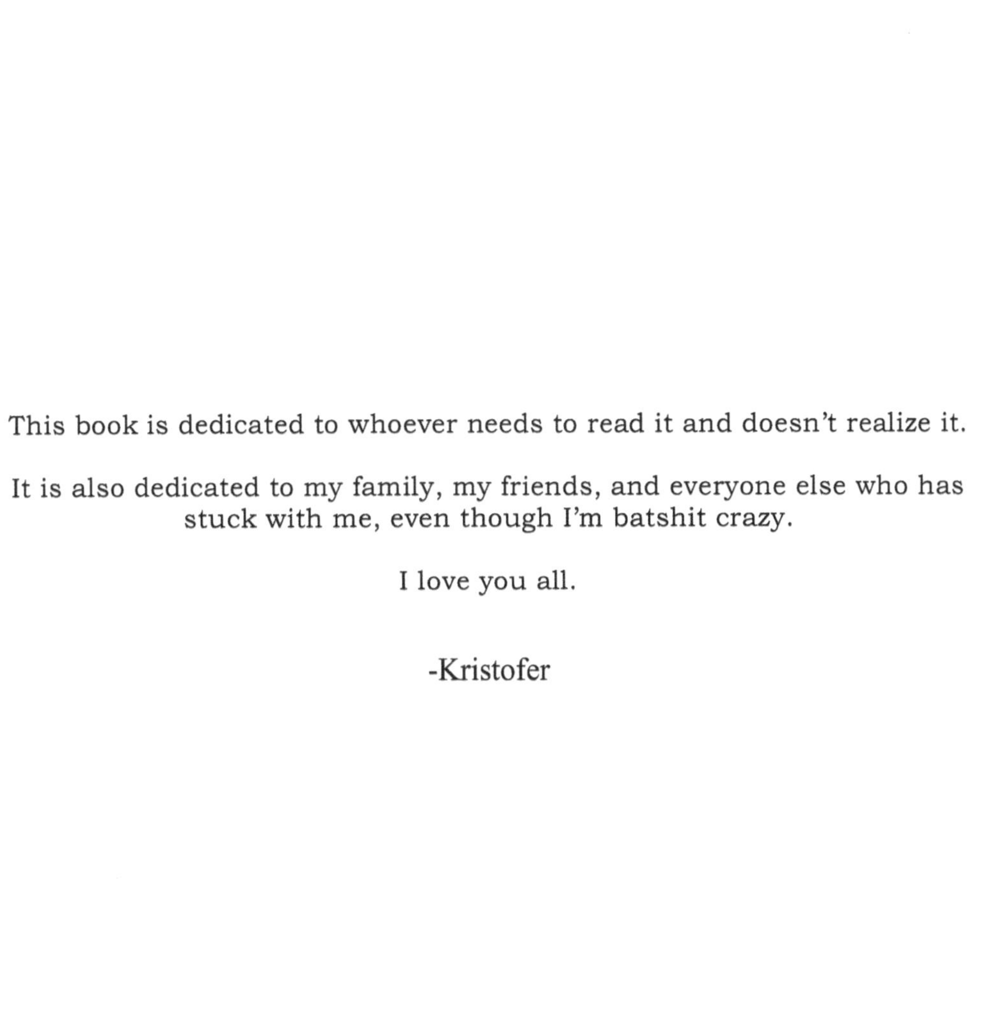

This book is dedicated to whoever needs to read it and doesn't realize it.

It is also dedicated to my family, my friends, and everyone else who has stuck with me, even though I'm batshit crazy.

I love you all.

-Kristofer

Forward

Life isn't easy, hell, it's not even fair.

The funny thing about life is sometimes it will cut you a break. I have had a rough life, by any means not as bad as some, but bad enough for me. My parents divorced when I was 3 years old. I love my parents but honestly, I'm glad that they separated. If they hadn't I don't know where my life would have taken me.

That's the thing about life, there are doors, doors that you open that sometimes lock behind you. I've never been one to believe in destiny or fate, but in that one rare instance that can change your mind, sometimes you have to let it.

I'm not going to sit here and bore you with my life story, of every event that led me to where I am now. I will however, give you the cliff notes version. Be forewarned, I tend to run in circles with my thoughts, take long tangents to prove a point. Stick with me though, and you may learn something about yourself, just as I have.

The Flood

The tears they fall like rain
The thoughts of you like lightning
My heart beats like thunder
Being apart from you is frightening
There is a storm inside of me
A hurricane is forming
These cloudy skies never seem to fade
My mind won't stop storming
You have always been my moon
You control my tide
Without you here in my life
From the tsunami I can't hide
It's been raining here inside my head
For nearly 30 days of night
I am treading water, losing strength
I don't know if I can keep up the fight
The tides keep getting higher
I'm forgetting how to swim
I submerge and start to drown
The lights are growing dim
As I slowly fall to darkness
I feel the ocean floor
My heart stops its beating
But at least I'm not hurting anymore

October 31st, 12:01 am

If you are reading this at this exact moment, know that I am reading it alongside you. Look up, you see that moon? I'm looking at it too. Underneath that big, bright moon, underneath all those bright and twinkling stars, I am looking at them with you, just like you always wanted us to. I'm just sorry it took so long.

I'm sorry for everything.

I wish that I could take it back I wish I could take every single ounce of pain I caused you back, I wish I could wipe away every single tear before they fell from your face.

Three years ago, today, at this very moment, you asked me to be your boyfriend. Two years later at that exact moment, I would ask you to be my wife. For those two moments, years apart, at the exact same time, I would be the happiest boy alive, but don't think that the time in between these two events in our timelines, I was ever any less happy.

In fact, in our entire first two years, give or take those first six months, I would be the happiest I would ever be in my life thus far, that is of course until you agreed to be my wife.

Now, you may be asking yourself, "What about our last year?"

That's a tough question.

We have faced many challenges, many trials, in not just our relationship, but our lives. Our last year together may prove to be our biggest challenge. You know our story, just as well as I do, but as everyone knows, there are two sides to every story.

If you are reading this like I hope that you are, please know that this is my side of the story. I wrote this book for myself and in some ways for you. I want you to understand exactly how I have felt having you in my life.

Chapter I

Tangents

As a kid, you have certain expectations of how things are supposed to be, expectations that are learned from television, movies, books, etc., expectations that are instilled in you by friends and family.

The thing is, everyone thinks differently, everyone views the world through different eyes, and sometimes our world view is fucked.

For all intents and purposes, this story is my story, and like every story it's about love. The thing about love is that it is a fickle bitch. You can't help who you fall in love with, just as you can't help who falls in love with you.

I don't want you to sit there and read the words on these pages and expect a love story, to expect a fairy tale ending. This book doesn't have one, in reality; this book doesn't even have a real ending. How can it though? I'm writing about my life, and I'm still alive. Alive in the truest sense of the word, my body is still functioning like it's supposed to. My heart is beating, blood is pumping through my veins, and air is still flowing through my lungs.

Beyond that though, I'm not really alive, and I haven't been for a long time. When you live your life like I have, it kinda makes it hard to really feel like you live in the land of the living. Growing up in a home where you get weekly beatings by your bastard of a stepfather it kinda makes you hate the world. It wasn't just me though, it was my mother too. Why anyone would ever want to hurt that saint of a woman, I can't imagine. Like anyone, she had her bad side, she had her moments of being a self-righteous bitch, but she loves me, and has always been the best mother she could be.

This in my eyes is exactly what she is, the best mother ever. I'm a momma's boy and saying that doesn't bring me even the smallest bit of shame. She helped me become the man that I am, this courteous, loving guy, who would give you the shirt off his back even in a blizzard. Not that I've ever experienced one living in Texas. I am that guy though, when I'm not, it's because of the rest of the world.

Assholes tend to do that to you though. They can really suck the life out of you, and make you a downtrodden, introverted douche bag. This is honestly how I've been lately. I don't want this book to just be how I view the world, especially with where my head is at. It's not pretty, hell, it's a head filled substitute Zoloft and substitute Vistaril. The Zoloft, because

—

I'm a bipolar, manic depressive who views the world for what it truly is, a pointless ball of shit. Filled with hate and anger, and money hungry politicians that decide how I get to live my life.

Don't get me wrong, I'm not some left-wing nut, who believes in conspiracy theories, but face it, it's true. America is run by greed, and our forefathers would be ashamed, as this was not their dream for our country. But alas, I am getting off subject, just like I said I would, sorry about that. I know that the world isn't all bad, and I have four nieces and two nephews to prove it. That doesn't prevent me from being a pessimistic narcissist though. Now the Vistaril, I honestly am not sure what this shit is supposed to do. My psychiatrist told me it is for anxiety, but I'm still pretty damn anxious all the time. Oh well, that's why I smoke cigarettes. Nothing like a cancer filled death stick to calm your nerves. If you're still reading this, I promise to try to move along with the story.

Maybe Chapter 2? Ha, who am I kidding, I'd be surprised if I ever even finish this book.

Chapter II
A Guilty Conscience

Suicide...

At some point in everyone's life, everyone thinks about it. About that bottle of pills, that bullet, that makeshift noose made out of an extension cord. Not everybody goes through with it though; some people get to that point, get ready to put that knife in their wrist, and bleed out, but stop. They get scared of that pain they feel as the blade pierces their skin.

That's what happened my first attempt at suicide.

That paring knife pierced my skin, and the pain alone stopped me. I guess I'm a bit of a wimp when it comes to pain. You're probably wondering why I tried in the first place, but like I said, this is about love. This love isn't the important one though, she isn't the love interest of this story, and I just wanted to at least appease your curiosity a little bit.

I guess I'll delve a little deeper for you, lucky you.

I was seventeen years old when I got my first real girlfriend, this was the girl I would lose my virginity to, the first girl I ever fell in love with, or at least thought I did. My heart was broken, I was sad, blah, blah, blah, I tried killing myself.

What's funny is the fact that the second attempt at suicide, now that I think about it, would actually set forth a string of events to lead to my third and last attempt.

The first one really doesn't count; I gave up half way through and barely have a scar. I would have to point it out to you for you to really even see it.

I honestly could have left the first attempt out and it wouldn't even affect the story all that much.

After high school, I was a bit of a douche bag, still feeling the anger and heart break of my first love. It really showed too, I lost a lot of friends and my mom kicked me out, but then again after years of abuse by her second husband, I wouldn't put up with my shit either.

Now, before you freak out, I never hit my mother. I would never hit her let alone any woman, but that didn't stop me from being a dick to her.

So, it's 2009, I'm nineteen, my mom kicked me out, and I move in to my grandmother's house with her and my father. My father is a good guy, but I just don't get along with him all that well. It's probably the fact that he and I are a lot alike. The same stubborn, bearded jerk, with a big heart, which wants the best for everyone, but goes about it the wrong way.

In the years of living with my dad and grandmother, and later my uncle, things progressed fairly normal, I guess...

The occasional hiccup did occur, but nothing major. I enlisted in the Navy, scored pretty high in my entry exams, was supposed to be a nuclear engineer, but that didn't really pan out. By that I mean, after a year of waiting to ship out to boot camp, I realized I really didn't want to be in the military.

Honestly, I'm just lazy, but at least I'm honest about it. Anyways, two years after I move in, my grandmother passed away. I took it pretty hard. She was an amazing lady, short and sweet, and probably the most loving person on the planet. Her death would later lead to my second attempt at suicide.

Now, losing a grandparent is a natural part of life, most people think nothing of it, grieve and move on. Not me though, but then again, I blamed myself for her death. Why? Well, I have insomnia, so my sleep schedule is pretty sporadic. Some days I sleep all day, some days I stay awake. The day she had her stroke was a day I slept.

We were the only two home that day, and my phone rings, with my dad telling me to get up and come into the living room.

I know now, that it wasn't my fault, but it didn't stop me then from blaming myself. I still don't know how long she was alone for before my dad found her, and who knows, maybe if I woke up earlier she could have made it through it.

It was December 30th, 2010 that she had her stroke, I remember that day because it was, or would have been my grandfather's birthday, had he not had died when I was little. She was hospitalized for a few weeks, until she passed in late January of 2011. I don't remember the day, because I still feel some blame.

The next few months are pretty hard; I was fighting guilt and working a new job. Somehow, I sprained my ankle. Why is that important? Well, I was hurt at work, so I was sent to a physician and given two bottles of prescription pain meds. If you're smart, you might have already figure out where I'm going with this.

April 30th, 2011, this was the day of my second attempt at suicide. I didn't really know what was different about this day, but it was a bad one. Something came over me, whether it was guilt or shame, depression, whatever I don't know. I just wanted to die.

So, I take both bottles, after googling the percentage of death by overdosing on both medications, just to make sure it would work. I lie in bed, watch Inception and fade into the deepest, blackest sleep of my life.

Chapter III

Dream Girl

This is where my story really begins, I'm sorry it took two chapters of rambling to get there.

So, where were we?

Oh, the deepest, blackest sleep of my life. Believe it or not, I wake up to the sound of my alarm going off.

Time to get up and go to work.

That's when it hits me, "Shit... I'm still alive."

I get out of bed, bowlegged for some odd reason, probably a side effect of the overabundance of pain meds in my system, and I take a shower. I get dressed and, in a stupor, I drive to work. I get there and tell my bosses, lying through my teeth, "I think I am having an allergic reaction to my medicine."

They send me to the clinic; I tell them I tried committing suicide. That's when they tell me, "We don't deal with suicides, you have to go to the hospital."

I get back into my car and drive to the emergency room and I tell them the same thing I told the clinic. They do my workup and after several hours of waiting I finally get in an ambulance and I am taken to the loony bin or a "Mental Health Rehabilitation Center."

God, that sucked, and it sucked the second time more so, but we're not quite there yet.

The good thing about ending up at "The Facility," was that I met her; My MJ, the love of my life.

When I got to The Facility, it was horrible. I felt like there was no point in being there and that I would lie my way to better health, just so that I could leave, and try once again to take my life. That is not what life had planned for me.

Like I said, sometimes life gives you a break.

I should probably mention something before I move forward with this story. Growing up, all throughout my life I had dreams, really the same dream. It was about this brown eyed, brown haired, pale, freckle faced girl. She only appeared at my lowest points, during my struggles and I could never figure out why. We are about to find out why.

Okay, back to my story. So, I'm processed into The Facility, I get to my room and I sleep. I wake up the next day, eat breakfast, talk to a psychiatrist, take some meds, and go to group therapy. This is when I see her; My MJ, the girl from my dreams.

People say different things about love, how they've experienced love at first sight and I had always thought it was just a bunch of bullshit. That it was just our mind filled with sexual desire. Yeah, I wanted to sleep with her, she's hot; I'm a guy, two plus two equals four. The thing is, that wasn't the first thing that popped in my head, seeing her was like an out of body experience, all I could see was her, like she was a blinding light in a pitch-black tunnel. I was in love and for the first time in my life I had hope.

If she wasn't there that day, at that exact time I was in the hospital I would not be alive.

I don't even remember that group, I don't remember the stories people told and what was even discussed, all I remember is this skinny, depressed girl, that was so beautiful, that even to this day, her image is forever burned into my mind. She looked dirty, in the sense that you could tell she hadn't showered. Her hair was greasy and knotted, there was a film of dirt on her skin, and blood and dirt under her fingernails. You could tell she went through hell before she got here.

She was sickly thin, she was so skinny, you could open a window and a light breeze would blow her away. Yet, even in her current state, she looked absolutely breathtaking, and you would have thought after being covered in dirt and grime, that she would smell terrible, but instead she smelled sweet, like the way it smells just before it rains.

I finally got the nerve to talk to her at one of our smoke breaks, I said something stupid, she laughed her sad laugh and smiled her big toothed smile, and right there in that moment, I fell even more in love.

I got to know her over the next few days; we exchanged stories and told tales of our shitty lives, of how I was abused and how she was too. Only her abuse, makes mine look like a pillow fight.

Still thinking about it makes my blood boil; it was the kind of abuse that would make you want to kill a man with your bare hands. At one point, they went to a drug deal, and he watched as the drug dealer raped her at gun point. Her fiancée was a bastard of man, calling him a man isn't even right, he was scum, the lowest form of life on the planet.

If she hadn't escaped when she had, she, without a doubt in my mind, would have been found somewhere on the side of the road, dead.

She was in recovery, from coke and crack, as well as almost every drug you can think of, from an abusive fiancée, she was bulimic. The bulimia from the point of view her fiancée brainwashed her to believe. She had natural beauty, she was perfect, and how could somebody possibly think otherwise?

How is being a literal twig, attractive? I'm sorry, but I like a woman with curves, and when MJ got back to a healthy weight, her beauty was amplified tenfold, the kind of beauty that would make any guy walk funny. The kind of beauty that would stop your heart.

After hearing about all of her pain, all of her struggles, it just made me fall in love with her more, it made me want her more, it made me want to fix her, to make her strong again.

Now there was another girl in The Facility, Kat, that I deeply care about and still do, but she was and is more like a big sister. Now Kat became inseparable from MJ. They were crazy close in the hospital. They did everything together and I mean everything. They barely ate together and they threw up together, they became sisters and their problems fused, but so did their strengths.

I say it was MJ that saved my life, but it was Kat as well.

They both helped me during that week-long stay, which felt like an eternity, but at least I had them. I felt loved by these two amazing girls and in that moment made me feel like I wanted to be alive, they made me feel hope again.

Their struggles became mine, and mine theirs, if not for them I would have left The Facility the same way I went in, instead I left with my head held high and a smile on my face.

We exchanged info MJ, Kat and I and one after the other left.

First MJ, then me and then a few weeks later Kat, but like I've said, this story is about me, about love, about MJ.

I kept in touch with MJ, but she just didn't seem interested in me in that way. I was more like a friend I guess, at least at first. I later found out that she liked me, but that she didn't want to date me because she felt like I knew too much about her and that it would create a problem in the relationship.

Again, later she told me that she fell in love with me just as I did her, that she too experienced love at first sight.

After I left the facility, I moved in with my mom for a few months, talked to Kat a lot and got ignored by MJ. Finally, about July 2011, I move back in with my dad, get another job and start college. In late October I get a message on Facebook from MJ's father, MJ was back in rehab and she wants to talk to me.

Wait a second, I skipped a part....

Chapter IV

That Was Awkward

It's now early October, I'm in school, working, living my boring life, when I randomly text MJ, to once again be ignored. She finally texts me back, and we have pretty long conversation, one that leads me to tell her that I like her. Even though in reality, I was absolutely in love with her, but then again, if I ever wanted to talk to this girl again, I wouldn't quite mention that.

I may be crazy, but I am not dumb.

She gives me the standard routine girls give, the usual text message of, "Awe, thank you."

God damn it! Friend zoned yet again!

A few days go by, and I get up enough nerve to ask her on a date, surprisingly enough she agrees, and then a little less surprisingly, blows me off. We wind up doing the same song and dance over and over of me saying, "Hey, let's do something together," with the usual reply of, "Okay, sure," with of course, the final outcome being once again... Blown off.

At this point, I'm getting pretty irritated, and in the process make one of the boldest moves of my life. Sometimes you have to go bold to get what you want.

I finally tell her what's what, that if she doesn't see me or go on a date with me that she can't talk to me anymore. As scary as that was for me, it had to be done. Believe it or not, she gives in and says okay, but once again I don't hear from her for a few weeks.

Great, she blew me off again.

Fearing that I scared her off, I just give up.

That is until I get a message on Facebook from her father, which went along the lines of, "Hey, this is MJ's father, she is in so and so rehab facility and wants you to come see her tomorrow."

I respond, "Okay, sure," not wanting to sound desperate, in reality I was jumping for joy, I finally get to see this girl I am head over heels in love with.

Okay, so you know how most people meet the parents of your significant other, and it's usually pretty weird? Yeah, imagine every single meeting of the other parents, stick them all together, and then put it in hell. I'm exaggerating of course, but you get the point, it was really fucking awkward.

Her parents and her grandparents were there.

I'm meeting the parents, as well as the grandparents, before ever even dating this girl.

I'm getting all kinds of questions about my life, like where I work, if I'm in school, the usual crap. The difference was, it was the grandparents asking most, if not all of the questions. I could tell that the grandfather had a stick up his butt and was judging my every word.

MJ winds up living with her grandparents at the beginning of our relationship and I find out that her grandfather is filthy rich. He gave her whatever she wanted, she had the chance for a full ride to an amazing college, that is until he found out she was dating me. He gave MJ the ultimatum of being taken care of the rest of her life or being cut from the will and staying with me.

She chose me, and he actually cut her out of the will.

What a bastard.

Anyways, back to the story.

It wasn't until they asked how I know her that things just got weird.

"So, how did you meet MJ?" The grandfather asks in the most condescending tone ever.

"Oh, uh... I met her at The Facility." I said in almost a whisper.

A few awkward seconds of silence later, they ask me why I was in The Facility and I tell them the truth.

One thing you have to know about me is that I'm honest, I don't lie, in fact I never lie, I don't like to lie and even if I did, I'm terrible at it. I have this habit of smirking oddly and giggling all throughout the lie.

Yeah, I guess I should never be a politician.

After telling them about my attempt at suicide in all the details possible, it just gets quiet, and stays that way until we are taken to visitation.

This whole ordeal happened in the lobby by the way.

Finally, after an eternity of waiting in the lobby, we are taken to visitation.

This wasn't as bad, they focused mainly on her; thank the invisible bearded man I don't believe in. I sat there awkwardly, not saying much of anything, the occasional yes or no, or nod in agreement.

After about an hour, they say that time is up. We are all saying our goodbyes and walk away, when MJ grabs my arm and pulls me aside and hugs me, kisses me slightly on my neck and grabs my crotch.

Yeah, that just happened.

She tells me she will call me later. That awkward meeting of the parents and grandparents would be on October 28th, 2011. That day still haunts my dreams. Which kinda sucks considering it is my older brother's birthday.

—

A few days pass and I finally receive a call from her.

11

Chapter V

A Most Eventful Hallows Eve

11:55 pm, October 30th, 2011, the night before Halloween.

I'm at a party for work, when she finally calls me.

"Hey, I missed you," she said in a soft, almost timid voice.

"I missed you too," I blurted out awkwardly as I always seem to do.

She giggles and says, "Um... When I get out, I want to fuck your brains out."

What the fuck? Did that really just happen?

"Uh... What?" I ask in almost a puberty stricken cracked voice, I sounded like a 13-year-old girl.

"You heard me," MJ said, this time in a much less timid voice, actually it was more of a command, it was forceful, and it made me instantly erect.

MJ had that effect on me, something about the sultry tones of her voice when she commanded me, the way she bossed me around. I don't know why, but I loved it, I still love it, I miss it.

I being the polite, mild mannered shy boy that my mother raised me to be, not trying to sound excited said, "Well, I don't really just sleep with girls for the heck of it. I do it when I'm in a relationship. I would really like to be in a relationship with you first."

I know, I know, I'm a pussy, but honestly, I wanted more than just sex with her. I wanted to be with her, I wanted her to be mine.

That and the fact that I had already gone through my man whore stage the summer of 2010. I had gone from the one girl I lost my virginity to in 2007 and never dating another girl until I met MJ. That didn't stop me from becoming a man whore though. Almost within a matter of months, I went from one girl to ten girls, two of which being within a 24-hour period, and another being my friend's mom.

I'm not proud of myself, in fact, I hurt a lot of girls that summer, but it felt good at the same time, I felt like I got revenge.

You'll find out why later.

And don't worry, karma catches up to me anyways, it always does, and it definitely did.

Back to my story.

Expecting her to laugh at me and to call me a pussy, her response was shocking, "Okay, then will you be my boyfriend?"

Me being single for four years, almost without hesitation, I said, "Of course!"

An awkward silence passes, and I look at the time.

"Oh! Look at the time, it's 12:01 am, Happy Halloween!"

So yeah, that's the story of how I got with MJ, she asked ME out! On Halloween no less! That has literally never happened, and probably never will again, girls just didn't talk to me like that. I always had to make the first move. Not with her though, not with MJ.

Chapter VI

M.J.

What you have to understand about MJ is that she is two different people.

And when I say two different people, I'm taking polar opposites. I don't mean this in like a "Sybil," split personality kind of way, more of how she acts around people. With me she was both, on one hand she was this upbeat, exciting, wild and crazy girl who would take what she wanted. On the other she was this soft spoken, shy, timid and just sweet person. The problem was that she would bounce back and forth between these two people, these two emotions and a lot of times, at the worst possible moment.

This story is about me, but to really understand MJ, I thought she at least deserved a chapter of her own.

Saying she is complicated would be saying Quantum Physics isn't.

She is the most complicated, mysterious, vexing woman I have ever had the pleasure of knowing and when we broke up for the last time, that mystery became much, much more, but more on that later.

I don't want to spoil the ending for you.

For the first six months of our relationship we lived 60 miles apart. She would visit me on the weekends and every single weekend I would break up with her. I'm a dick, I know. She would always take me back though. What you have to understand about me is that...

Wait a minute, this chapter is about her, not me, I'll come back to that in the next chapter, I promise.

After six months of this routine, she moved into my dad's house with me, I stopped trying to break up with her at this point, and again, you will find out why in the next chapter.

No peeking!

Things were good, but they were touchy, I worked and she didn't, but then again, she wasn't ready. She was still fighting her depression as well as her addictions.

Honestly though, as tough as it was, I didn't mind, I loved having her be there when I got home. It wasn't until May of 2012, that I realized just how bad her alcoholism was. Aside from the abuse she received from her fiancée, aside from the drugs, the rape, MJ had lost a lot of people, a lot of people she cared about. Family and friends, all died one after the other, and this happened all throughout our relationship.

Dealing with that kind of abuse and that kind of loss, it really fucks with your head, so it's understandable for her to want to drink her pain away. She had been clean off of drugs for just over a year, but she was still drinking, I didn't really think much of it, because she told me that it was the drugs that she had a problem with.

I was stupid for believing that, I know.

It didn't really bother me until it became a noticeable problem in our relationship. What made it worse was that I was helping to supply her with some of the alcohol, I helped fuel her alcoholism. She started drinking more and more and it got to the point of where she started doing stupid things with her friends.

It got to the point where she ignored me and would get angry with me for no reason. We were at my mother's house in May, just visiting. My mother left for the weekend and we were going to stay the night. Well, we got in a huge fight, I don't even remember why, it was something stupid.

I finally told her, I couldn't do it anymore, I couldn't be with her if she was going to destroy herself. We got in the car and I was taking her home. She called her brother and told him what was going on and how she was losing the most important person in her life. That's when it hit me, she needed help and I was running away, which is ironic because she did the same thing to me, but again, I'm getting ahead of myself.

As we are driving, I tell her, "I want you to get help. I will be there every step of the way, but don't do it for me, do it for you. I can't be with you if you keep destroying yourself."

She checked herself back into that same facility we met in and got better.

Well, at least she stopped drinking.

She always has had a problem with addiction, when she couldn't have one thing, she would move on to another. This time it was sex. Don't worry, she never cheated on me, she just had a sexual drive that was almost animalistic. It got to the point that I could barely walk and it hurt to put boxers on. Talk about chaffing, I wish I had learned about lube sooner. Not that I am complaining though, the problem with this is that mistakes are bound to happen. She got pregnant but miscarried, this would later happen again.

I only found out recently how many times it happened, she only ever told me about two, but there were four more times that it happened. Six miscarriages.

Looking back, it explains a lot of her depression during our time together. She was and is a beautiful person inside and out, as time went on I could see that light that she had, grow dim. I blame myself for a lot of what happened, but a lot of it was out of my control. Really, the one thing you need to know about MJ is that I love her more than life itself, and at one point she loved me the same. Loved being the key word.

Backtracking

Keeping my promise from last chapter, I will explain a few things for you.

During the first six months of my relationship with MJ, I broke up with her every weekend. The thing you have to understand about me is that I got hurt a lot by girls growing up, I always got shot down, and a lot of times in the worst possible ways, and because of this I had a lot of trust issues.

With MJ, as much as I love her, I always had this doubt in my mind that I couldn't talk to her without being judged, that I would be judged by her just like I was with the other girls. This is one of the key factors of our eventual final break up, but again, more on that later.

I'm not saying that any of my failed relationships or failed attempts at talking to a girl weren't my fault, because that would be a big fat lie. I'm not the perfect person, I make mistakes just like everyone else, but I never go out of my way to hurt anyone.

That's what most, but not all, of these girls did. Some of them I never even got a chance to date, some of them I just showed affection to and was tortured for it.

I'll give you an example. Eloise.

Eloise was this gorgeous red head that I was in drum line with. Oh man, I loved her without really knowing who she was. I tend to do that a lot by the way, falling in love with beautiful woman who are nice to me. Anyways, one day I write Eloise a poem, I type it out, I print it and give it to her after school and just walk away. Big mistake.

I go to school the next day and everyone in the band hall is laughing at me. I look around and there are hundreds of copies of my poem all over the walls and doors. I was devastated and because of it I later quit band, oh well, I sucked anyways (according to one of my instructors).

I would go through high school and face a similar series of events that would make me pretty much not trust another woman again. As you know though, I do get my revenge against the fairer of the sexes.

I wouldn't trust another woman until MJ, which would leave me single for the next few years. As I have said, the first six months of my relationship with MJ would have countless breakups. It wasn't until that sixth month that I realized I could trust her, that she really did love me.

She was over for the weekend and as per usual we got into a fight over something stupid. I told her to leave, to get out and never come back, she was heartbroken, she was devastated, and I could see the tears flowing down her face onto her favorite yellow jacket. After she left, after seeing those tears flow from her eyes, I realized that I was a dumbass.

I called her and begged her to take me back.

She did so without hesitating and from that moment on I knew I could talk to her about anything, I could trust her no matter what happened.

That didn't stop me from fucking things up anyways.

Caution, Road Bumps Ahead

MJ and I lived with my dad for a while longer.

My dad was selling the house, but that didn't take hold for a few months. Finally, in January of 2013, I get a call from my dad saying, "I have been made an offer on the house, you have 48 hours to get your shit out and leave."

The house was finally being sold, but he didn't want us to live with him anymore, he felt that MJ and I were dead weight. We move in with MJ's parents, but it wasn't just them, her brother Joe was there with his fiancée Krystal, as well as Joe's son from a previous marriage and Joe and Krystal's new born daughter.

MJ and I slept in the living room on the floor for half of our stay there; the only time we didn't sleep on the floor in those first few months was when Joe's son was with his mother. We were then allowed to sleep in his bed, his tiny little trundle bed. It wasn't until later in the summer that we were upgraded to an air mattress in the living room. We finally got tired of it and decided we were going to go to school and move upstate. My mom set us up in an apartment, which we couldn't afford, even with our student loans.

What was worse, was that I got sick with bronchitis, got fired from the job I just got hired on to and missed so much school that I had to drop out for the semester. I forgot to mention that the last time I was in school I was diagnosed with diverticulitis and had to drop out then due to the time it would take to heal.

Anyways, I reapplied for the spring semester of 2014 and got denied my financial aid. MJ also got sick during this time and had to drop out; she was also denied her financial aid for the next semester.

I was lucky to get another job, but I just didn't make enough money to make ends meet, so once again we had to pack up and move back in with her parents, this time was much, much worse.

I keep forgetting parts of the story, the Christmas of 2013, Joe and Krystal announce to MJ's parents that Krystal is once again pregnant. They were not happy about it in the least.

Back to the story, the house was loud, tempers were high and fights ensued. Due to Krystal being pregnant once again, MJ's parents were not happy. It became a daily struggle to avoid any conversation becoming a confrontation; it was nearly impossible to get any sleep and after a few months of living there, MJ, Joe, Krystal and I decided to get a place of our own.

BIG. FUCKING. MISTAKE.

Beginning of the End

This is where the end began, obviously pointed out by the title of this chapter.

Everything started out fine.

MJ got a new job working overnight as a stocker, I was able to transfer jobs and everyone held up their end and we were doing okay. We weren't living comfortably, but we were fine. The first few months went by like clockwork, this wouldn't last long though.

I don't blame anyone for the way things ended up, like I have said before, sometimes life cuts you a break. This was not one of those times.

May 2014, Krystal takes her leave from work, as the new baby boy was coming soon. We were down an income and because of this we struggled, we barely got by. Bills started piling up and eventually we got behind, too behind.

Honestly at this point we should have all moved out and each couple should have gotten their own place. The problem was, because we were so far behind we couldn't afford to break the lease, so we tried to stick it out.

We should not have done that.

The pressure got to MJ and I and we started fighting a lot.

What made things worse was that because she worked over night and I worked during the day, we never saw each other. When we did, we fought, and we fought about anything and everything.

The time apart, the fact we never saw each other, the fighting, all of it made me sink back into my depression. And this would become the second worst depression of my life.

The first we will get to in the next chapter.

I stopped talking to her completely, I tried for a while to explain to her how I felt and she looked into getting another job, one that would allow us to have more time together, one that wouldn't set us apart so much.

 Eventually she gave up on that idea.

She felt that her job was more important.

It's understandable, we needed the money and the other job was a downgrade in pay. I viewed it then as: her job was more important than me, more important than our relationship, and that's when I really shut down.

I haven't mentioned it before, but I am an avid gamer, gaming is my second love, MJ being the first.

I shut myself away in my video games, and in the process slowly but surely pushed her away. She started hanging out with people from work; she started coming home later and later. Then it became she wouldn't come home on her breaks. She started drinking again and even started smoking pot at work.

It got to the point of, she would get home from work, and we would go to sleep. I would wake up and go to work and then come home and she would immediately leave for work. This process continued for about a month.

Friday, September 19th, 2014. This was and for all intents and purposes the last day she ever told me she loved me. This would be the day that would change everything. This will be the day that I lose her, before actually losing her.

One of her coworkers, Richard, needed a ride home from work. I thought nothing of it, as she had given him and other coworkers rides home before.

This time was different though, Richards's apartment was being sprayed for bugs, so he couldn't go home for several hours. She picked him up about seven am and keep in mind, Friday was our only day that we had off together.

She didn't get home until seven pm.

She spent the whole day with this guy, I knew something was wrong, but I was still so shut down, that I didn't push it, I didn't pursue it.

I should have, I should have never said I was okay with her spending that much time with Richard without me, because it wasn't okay. She got home and told me that Richard had invited her to a wedding for one of his friends; I stupidly said it was okay, even though it really wasn't. Now the wedding wasn't for another week, but that wouldn't matter anyways.

Sunday, September 21st, 2014, 1:35 am. I hear my phone go off, it's a text from MJ, and it says, "Idk how much more I can take of this... I never see you anymore..."

Conversation ensues, discussions are had, I tell her I love her and that I want to fix this. I tell her that we need to change something; she agrees and says that if we don't, she doesn't feel like it will work anymore.

Monday, September 22nd, 2014, 5:53 am. Another text from MJ, "Richard needs a ride home." I tell her okay and that I love her and that I will see her when she gets home.

Tuesday, September 23rd, 2014 3:13 am. Another text, the last important text from MJ. "Is it okay if I drop Richard off again? When I come home I think we should talk."

I respond, "OK"

The End

Hearing the words leave her mouth broke my heart and froze me in place.

It's almost as if I went on autopilot.

She told me that it wasn't working anymore, that she felt like we were too different, and that somewhere along the way we grew apart.

I agreed with her.

I froze, I told her I agreed with her, when in reality, I did not.

Every fiber of my being was screaming to move, to grab her, to tell her I love her, but instead I lied. The only lie I ever told her, I was always honest with her, always, and I lied. I said it, and she believed it, I told a lie. Losing her is what I regret the most, but that lie is a close second.

We acted fine afterwards, like nothing really happened and said that we would be friends. She even gave me a goodbye blow job and told me the thing she would miss most was my cock.

She even asked if we could be fuck buddies.

After a while she fell asleep and I had my mom come get me for lunch, I told her what had happened and how I was okay with it. I was feeding her the same bullshit MJ fed me, the same bullshit I fed myself. We talked for about an hour, ate our food and she took me home. I walked inside and get in that bed next to MJ, when it finally hit me, when it finally sunk in.

I didn't want this, I never wanted this.

I picked up my notebook and wrote her telling her exactly that, I told her in so many words that I didn't want to lose her, that I couldn't lose her.

I woke her up and made her read it and then we talked.

Another thing about MJ is that when she sets her mind to something, when she makes a decision, it's final. She has always been stubborn that way.

It didn't matter how I felt anymore, for her, hearing me say those words, that I agreed with her, that was it. She told me that the day she spent with Richard, she felt like we used to, that I just wasn't the boy she fell in love with anymore, that I was just gone and that she wanted to cheat on me with Richard, but that she didn't. She wanted to, but she didn't.

We always told each other if we got to the point of wanting to cheat, that we would rather leave one another than actually cheat, and that is exactly what she did.

After talking for a little while longer we went back to sleep, she left for work that night, which gave me a lot of time to think. When she got home that morning I was so angry, the angriest I have ever been in my life. I didn't understand how after 3 years of being together, after a year of being engaged...

Oh, by the way we got engaged on Halloween of 2013.

A few months before I asked her to marry me, we were in our college apartment in our living room, and "our song" came on, Justin Timberlake's Mirrors. I grabbed her and we slow danced for the entirety of the song.

Feeling her so close to me in my arms, her head against my chest, hearing her breathe, the way she smelled of vanilla; I knew in that moment that I wanted to spend the rest of my life with her. In that moment I was totally and utterly blissful. I never wanted to let that moment go, I never wanted to let her go. That was and is my favorite memory of us...

I didn't understand how after almost 3 years of being together, after almost a year of being engaged that it was over?

How could she do that to me?

I was so mad at her; I blamed her for all of it.

It wasn't until later, that I realized most of it was my fault. I talked to her at first, then I yelled, then I screamed and called her names. It breaks my heart that I did that, I didn't know what to do or how to fix it. Again, I told her to leave and to never come back. Only this time, she wouldn't.

Nine Minutes Till

The next few days I sat alone in my room, lost in my own world again and I knew she wasn't coming home. I texted her now and then, trying to get her back, but it was in vain, until one day I told her I wanted to talk to her in person, to end it officially.

That is what I meant to do at least, but instead I begged and I pleaded for her to come back.

We talked for a while and I asked her if she still loved me, she told me yes, I asked her if she felt like we could ever get back together again, she said no. The tears came flowing down my face like rain during a thunderstorm.

I said, "That's all I needed to know," and I walked away.

I got in my car, I looked in the rearview mirror, and she was gone.

I drove home, misty eyed, with a pain in my chest. I couldn't be there anymore; I couldn't be in this house that destroyed my relationship, in this house that broke my heart.

I had my mom come help me pack; an hour and a half later I was gone.

I packed what I needed, I packed a few things I wanted, all in all, I packed my whole life into 3 cardboard boxes and a wooden chest.

The drive to my dads was the longest drive I ever took, I had driven it so many times before just to visit, but this was different. I was leaving my whole life behind, and I blamed her for everything, but I couldn't bring myself to hate her.

I now know why, why I couldn't hate MJ, why I couldn't blame her.

It was my fault, I try to push it all on her so that I can feel less shitty, but at the end of the day, it was my fault. I may have tried, but I didn't try hard enough, I lost her and it was my own damn fault. I can't blame life for it ending, but I can blame life for throwing out the obstacles, but in the end, I was the one who shut the door.

Over the course of the next few days I settled in with my dad, I transferred back to my old job and I was trying to get back to normal. Things felt normal, I was sad, I missed her, but life was starting to feel normal.

Sunday, October 5th, 2014, 1:30 am.

This was the hardest day so far, harder days are ahead, but this was definitely the day things started to unravel and go downhill. This would lead me to the worst depression of my life, and it all happened within an hour and twenty-one minutes.

I was missing MJ really bad, so I started snooping on her Facebook to look at pictures.

I should never have done that.

I was scrolling through her page when I saw it, when I saw the post that would push me over the edge. She was in a relationship with Richard.

The date said September, 22nd, we didn't even break up until September 23rd. This destroyed me. How after 3 years could she leave me and immediately be with someone else? How could that even be possible? It's as if she planned to break up with me for him and that made me feel worthless. And on top of that she lied. She told me that they would never be together, that she didn't leave me for him, and that she would stay single for a while.

Sunday, October 5th, 2014, 2:16 am.

I text her asking how should could already be with someone else, I asked her how she could do this to me. Did I mean nothing to her? She never responds.

Sunday, October 5th, 2014, 2:39 am.

I text her, I call her, I want to hear her voice, I want to hear her voice one last time. I want to talk to her; I leave her a voicemail begging her to call me back, pleading for her to come back to me. She never responds.

Sunday, October 5th, 2014, 2:51 am, I text her....

"Goodbye"

Chapter XII

3:00 am

Smoke fills my car.

My chest hurts, I blacked out for only a second.

When I come to, I look around for a few things and I get a phone call. It's MJ...

It doesn't go well.

I get out of the car and look at the damage, it's hard to see, it's really dark out, and the moon is nowhere to be seen. I hear sirens in the distance and I start to see flashing lights on the opposite side of the freeway.

"Man, I want a cigarette," pops in my head.

One cop car pulls up, the police officer points his flood light at me, and I'm sitting on the trunk of my car.

"Sir, are you injured?" The police officer asks me.

"I'm fine," I say, "My chest hurts though and I can't find my cigarettes anywhere."

He begins asking me questions, the usual questions cops always ask you. Have you been drinking? Was there anyone else in the vehicle? No, it was only me...

Let me back up.

Sunday, October 5th, 2014, 2:51 am.

I text her, "Goodbye."

I'm sitting in my car, I light up what I thought was going to be my last cigarette and I start the engine.

I drive, looking for the perfect spot. I get on the freeway, and I push the pedal to the floor. I'm accelerating.

60.

80.

100.

120.

140.

My steering wheel starts to shake; the cars beside me look like blurs, the governor kicks in and locks my speed at 140 miles per hour. I look around, there are no cars in sight, I turn a hard left, and the world around me is spinning.

—

I regain control, only I'm driving on the wrong side of the road, I speed up, passing the cars around me. Even at 140 miles per hour, I have complete control over my vehicle, I don't know if it was just the adrenaline kicking in or what, but I felt like I was in a car chase in some spy movie.

Finally, no more cars in sight, I turn a hard right, and again at 140, spin out.

Why wouldn't my car just flip already? Why couldn't I just die?

I once again regain control and I speed back up to 140 mph. That's when I see it, that's when I know. Perfect...

Sunday, October 5th, 2014. 3:00 am. The last hard left I took would send my car at full force into a cement wall; the impact was enough to crush the front end of my car into what looked like a can of sardines with a pull tab. The impact would send me into a daze. I come to and I am pissed.

"WHAT THE FUCK!" I scream, "WHY THE FUCK CAN'T I JUST FUCKING DIE?"

I scrounge around the floorboard of my car looking for three things:

My glasses, check!

My phone, check!

My cigarettes, where are my cigarettes?

I almost fucking died and all I can think about is my god damned cigarettes.

How sad is that?

I hear a vibrating sound followed by the theme song from Star Wars. It's MJ.

"Hello," I belt out angrily.

"What's wrong?" She asked in a semi concerned voice.

"I can't even FUCKING kill myself," I scream.

"Why not, what do you mean?" She asks this time in a more concerned tone.

Anger flowing through me like fire, I belt out, "Because I just tried three fucking times, and I failed. I wrecked my car going 140 mph, and I'm still fucking alive! What the fuck?!" Almost in a whisper, as if she is scared of the answer, she asks, "Why? Why would you try to kill yourself?"

Disgusted by the question, that I knew she already knew the answer to, in the scariest yell I have ever made I say, "WHY? WHY THE FUCK DO YOU THINK? HOW CAN YOU ALREADY BE WITH SOMEBODY ELSE? AFTER THREE FUCKING YEARS? DID I MEAN NOTHING TO YOU, YOU FUCKING BITCH?"

She hangs up on me.

Fast forward a bit, back to the cop and his questions.

"What happened," he asks me.

I tell him my story, of how I tried to kill myself by slamming into a cement wall at 140 mph.

I tell him, "Put me in a fucking loony bin already!"

"Why?" He asks concerned.

"Because I want to die and I can't even do that!"

After a few seconds of silence, I ask him, "Will you look for my cigarettes; I can't seem to find them."

He searches my car and finds them, but he can't find the lighter. After a few more minutes of waiting, more cop cars pull up, a fire truck is in the distance and I can hear the sirens of the ambulance. One by one, each police officer, fire fighter and paramedic ask me questions, and one by one I ask each one for a lighter.

Apparently, nobody smokes anymore.

Seatbelts

Several hours later, after being poked and prodded with needles, after x-rays of my chest and CT scans of my head and body, I find out nothing is wrong with me physically.

"Thank god, you were wearing your seatbelt," the doctor said.

"Yeah," I reply sarcastically.

Out of all the things I could forget to do that night, I forget the most important one, taking off my seatbelt.

Looking back now I am glad I forgot, I wouldn't be here otherwise. I'm thankful I forgot, as miserable as I am, I am still alive. I walked away from that car wreck with nothing more than a bruise from my left collar bone all the way to my right hip, a skinned knee and a light abrasion on my right wrist.

No scars whatsoever, no broken bones, not even a scratch.

I'm honestly in more pain now, after spending hours writing this book, and now typing the rough draft. I am so lucky. I don't believe in god or angels, but that day somebody or something was watching over me.

If there is any lesson to be learned from this, it has to be:

Wear

your

fucking

seat

belt!

The Looney Bin

Being in the emergency room I was given two choices, "Willingly go into the mental health facility" or "Have your rights taken away and go into the mental health facility."

So, I went to the mental health facility.

Like I mentioned earlier, this place was worse than the first, much worse. It took a day and a half just to see a psychiatrist, and when I did, it was for two minutes. I wouldn't see him again until the day before I left, which would be to tell me, "You leave tomorrow."

I couldn't sleep from the pain of my chest, but they wouldn't give me any pain meds and they wouldn't give me sleeping pills either. I think the one good thing that happened in that godforsaken hell hole was I had to go back to the ER for more tests, I was having extreme chest pain and heart palpitations, the EKG at The Loony Bin would show some irregular levels and the staff thought I was going to have a heart attack.

They gave me some nitroglycerin and sent me to the hospital with a member of staff to watch me. Betty.

Betty was gorgeous, she was the kind of beauty that made people double take and I get to sit alone in a room with Betty for hours. It made me miss MJ a lot less, but honestly Betty was just a distraction of the pain I felt in missing MJ.

Another lesson you can learn from this is always have health insurance, I did not this time around.

I really didn't get help in The Looney Bin.

I was only covered for two days through the state, yet I stayed for four.

I'm still scared to get all of my hospital bills. Just from the ambulance rides alone, I know I'm going to be in debt for a long time.

I met some interesting people in this place, but I didn't learn any of their stories. I didn't really talk to anyone this time. I remember a couple names, but that is about it. The thing is, the whole reason I was there, was for me, and I realized it this time.

The first time I was in a place like this, when I was in The Facility, I focused so much on everyone else, I forgot my own problems. I didn't fix them, I forgot them and I tried to fix everyone else's. It's good to help others, but sometimes you need to focus on yourself. That's exactly what I did this time, that is, when I wasn't thinking about MJ.

—

I wrote, not a lot, I mainly slept, when I was awake I reflected on myself. I still thought about MJ a lot, I still do. It's hard to let go of someone you loved for so long.

To an almost twenty-five-year-old man, three years is a long time. That's about an eighth of my overall time on this shit ball of a planet. If there is one thing I can learn from my stay at The Loony Bin, it is that I never want to go back.

Goodbye MJ

The day before I left The Loony Bin, I called MJ; I fought myself for days to not call her. I would avoid walking near a phone, just for the fact I knew I would call her.

I gave in and finally called her.

Hearing her voice again made me feel happy again, tears of joy streamed down my face. Even though she had somebody new, it filled my heart with pure joy just to hear her say my name. I told her I was getting out the next day and I asked if it would be okay if I called her, she said yes. The next few hours seemed like days. I couldn't sleep, I wanted out of there so bad, I wanted to hear her voice again, and I wanted to see her.

Wednesday, October 8th, 2014, 6:30 pm.

I got out today, I was supposed to leave at 11:30 am, and it is now 6:30 pm. I am so tired of waiting. Waiting to see more doctors, waiting for people to tell me it's time to leave. Thank god my dad picked me up; I couldn't stand to be in that place for one more second. I'm finally home. MJ is supposed to call me, or wait, am I supposed to call her? I'll just text her, hmm... no response. Maybe I'll call her, hmm... Voicemail.

Wednesday, October 8th 2014, 10:15 pm.

The phone finally rings.

"Hello," I say,

"Hi," she says.

We would talk for 2 hours, 27 minutes and 39 seconds. She would at this point tell me to come over the next day.

So, I do.

I have my mom pick me up the next day and take me to her parents' house. Over the next 5 days, I stayed at her parents' house, we would talk, I would beg her to come back to me, she would tell me she loves me, that she wants to be with me, but that she needs a better reason than to just be with me, to leave Richard.

We would talk more, she would try to convince me to go back to her room and fuck her.

She would do this several times during my stay with her.

Almost giving in every time, I would tell her no, I couldn't bring myself to let her cheat, even as much as I wanted to, I couldn't be that guy.

She would then go on to tell me she slept with Richard, that she might be pregnant, that it might be his.

As much as you would think that would've hurt me, it didn't.

I didn't care, I wanted her back.

Over the next few weeks I would talk to her, I would beg and plead with her every day to come back to me and to no avail, she wouldn't.

I would receive threatening texts from Richard, with him struggling to put sentences together, to even use proper English, to struggle to make me crack.

With his second-grade reading and writing level, he was just no match for my wit.

I tore him a new one.

My wit once again would come out ahead, but wit doesn't get the girl.

MJ starts to ignore me, she won't respond to my call or texts.

I would send a billion texts and call her a billion times. Yes, I'm exaggerating, but for a better sense of what it felt like, to me it was a billion.

She finally responded.

She told me to stop trying.

That no matter what I did, I would never get her back.

I wrote her a letter, I told her I wanted to read it to her, after hours of persuasion, she finally gave in. After about five and half pages of the six-page letter I wrote, telling her that even if she was pregnant, even if it was his, that I didn't care, that even if I had to raise somebody else's baby, I just wanted to be with her.

She tells me to stop reading, she isn't pregnant.

She tells me she doesn't want to hear anymore, she doesn't want to get back with me ever, that how could she after I broke her heart? That she wants to sever ties and that I shouldn't beg her to come back anymore, because it would just make her hate me more.

How could she hate me?

What did I do that was so bad, that she hated me?

How did I break her heart, when she broke mine?

I would continue for the next day or so to try to talk to her, until I finally realized I had to let go, that this was destroying me. This was the day before yesterday.

Monday, October 20th, 2014, 8:49 pm.

After deciding that I had to her to let her go, I would send her one last text, but before she would read it she would call me one last time.

Yesterday, Tuesday, October 21st, 2014, 6:29 am. Buzz... Buzz... Buzz... I awake to the sound of the Star Wars theme playing.

It's MJ. Why is she calling me?

"Hello?" I answer, puzzled.

"Hi, I just saw that you called and was returning your phone call. I just want you to know that I will always be here for you." She said, sounding tired, as it was nearing the end of her shift.

"Did you get my text?" I asked her, the uncertainty of that question making me nervous, feeling the confusion as well from hearing her last statement.

"No," she replies, "I haven't checked my phone in a while."

Fighting the urge to ask her one last time to come back to me, I say, "Read my text, goodbye MJ."

I hang up.

Monday, October 20th, 2014, 8:49 pm.

"So, I've decided that I'm not going to talk to you anymore. It's not good for me. I love you and I don't want to let you go, but the thing is, I can't push you to be with me. I can't force you. And that is what I have been doing this whole time. I'm so sorry I hurt you and I will always regret it. I will always love you and I won't ever let you go from my heart, but I just can't keep doing this to myself. It's too hard. I didn't want to let go of you, because I felt like if I did, you would never come back to me, that you would never speak to me again. That you would completely fall out of love with me. I hope that someday we can be together again, that we can fix our problems, but I can't force it on you. I am sorry that I have been pestering you, this just has been hard on me. I love you and I wish you the best in life."

Fin?

It's funny, I started this book today.
My mom told me to write a book, so I did just that.
I never finish anything, I always give up.
I even said in the very first chapter that I doubt I would even finish.
Yet here I am.

I have written this whole thing, in less than a day. I guess I'm just bored. Letting go of MJ, is going to be hard, who knows maybe I never will, but like I said there is not fairy tale ending in this book, but that doesn't mean I won't fine one.

Always and forever yours,
Kristofer

Chapter XVII

Manic

Chapter Sixteen was originally the last chapter, but as I have said before I am a bipolar manic depressive with anxiety issues and I tend to bounce around a lot.

After finishing Chapter Sixteen, the next few days I would be a little manic, by a little I of course mean my head was all over the place.

October 22nd, 2014.

Today feels like a good day.

After writing my book I am now typing up the rough draft and making edits. It takes me several hours to type everything up and to organize some of my thoughts. Overall, I feel better today, writing my story has really helped and I feel as though I may finally be on the path to let her go.

October 23rd, 2014.

FUCK TODAY.

It's been a month to the day since she left me.

Once again, I resort to snooping on MJ's Facebook page.

I am missing her desperately.

Having deleted all of her pictures from my computer and phone, this is the only way I can see her face again.

As I look through her pictures, I see a collage she made for us after I proposed to her.

She wrote the following: "On this day, October 31st, 2013 my boyfriend of 2 years asked me to marry him and of course I said yes. This is by far the best day of my life. My best friend, my soul mate and my one and only. I am beyond words right now. I love you Kristofer Dalton West."

Seeing this post again broke my heart to pieces all over again.

Not wanting to bother MJ any more than I already have, I write down how I feel.

"Today is a hard day for me. A month ago, today, my would be future wife left me. I can't believe it has already been a month. I'm trying my hardest not to break down and I'm failing miserably. I love her so much and now she's gone from my life. She used to think of me in the kind of way that you often see people in love in movies look at each other. 8 more days to our would be three-year anniversary. It breaks my heart. I pushed her away from me and when I wanted to finally get up and fight it was too late. I fucked up and I will regret it for the rest of my life. I love

———

her so much and I know that I will never feel her love again, I will never feel her lips against mine. It kills me inside, I feel as though my heart is black and is crumbling to ash."

Writing this honestly made me feel worse, so I wind up texting her anyways.

October 24th, 2014, 12:34 am.

"This is unbearable. I know I shouldn't be texting you. I know I shouldn't because it hurts you just as much as it hurts me. I love you, I wish that I didn't, but I can't help it. I can't help that you are who and what I think about every second of every day. Hell, even in my dreams you are there. I can't have you in the real world but at least I have you in my dreams. I keep saying maybe someday... Maybe someday we can fix our problems, maybe someday we can be together again, but someday just seems so far away. I can't believe it has been a month since you broke up with me, it seems like only yesterday that you said you would marry me. 8 days. 8 more days and we would have been together 3 years. 1 year and 8 days and we would have been married. It kills me to think about it, but it's all I ever seem to think about. I'm sorry if I'm bothering you, you can ignore me if you want. It's probably best that you do and I'm sorry if this upsets you. It's just that no matter how hard I try, I just can't seem to get over you. I don't know that I ever will."

October 24th, 2014, 3:53 am.

Tired, and manic, I come up with a plan, one last try to get her back. I decide to send her a copy of my book in the mail in a rough draft form, with instructions not to read it until 12:01 am on October 31st, 2014 and to go outside.

150 Percent

In a way, I view this book as our love story.

In a way I don't.

I also view it as our falling out of love story.

How it ends is up to you, just as how it began was. The way I look at it, you have always been the dominate force in our relationship. I once told you that I felt like a relationship should be 100/100, instead of 50/50, because divorce is 50/50.

I told you I felt like for us, it was more 100/50, you being the 50. I have realized now that you have always been the 100 and that I was the 50. I was devoted to you 100 percent, but the relationship only 50%. You were always 100% to both. For that I am sorry, I am sorry for a lot of things and the list itself could be a book, but I'm not going to say I'm sorry anymore. Instead, I am just going to ask you for your forgiveness.

MJ, after everything we have been through, after everything that I have done, can you ever forgive me? I didn't write this book to get you back, that was never my intention, it was for me. Those first sixteen chapters are mine, they are for me, they were and are to help me cope with losing you. These last four chapters though, are for you, the next one for us, the next one for the ending of our story or maybe just the beginning.

The Future

I'll leave it up to you.

Part Two

Forward

July 2nd, 2018

I had a hard time sleeping last night, for some reason MJ popped into my head, along with this book.

I'm not sure why, but there they were, these thoughts that wouldn't go away.

I was thinking about the past, about everything that transpired all those years ago, but it didn't hurt like it used to. Yes, I was sad, but it didn't hurt anymore.

I've been sad a lot lately, maybe it's because I've been lonely, maybe it's the reoccurring depression, maybe it's for some other reason.

I honestly couldn't tell you.

The thing is, I've learned to cope with this sadness that reoccurs in my life off and on. Yeah, I still have the odd suicidal thought now and then, but these thoughts aren't anything that I would ever act on.

When it happens, I kind of ride it out like a wave, take a breath, and move on. When it's really bad, I know I have people in my life I can call any time, day or night.

That's the thing with depression, you have to have a great support system, and you have to have even better coping skills.

I'm not sure why I'm continuing this book, but it feels like something I have to do. I feel like I have more of my story to tell.

Maybe someone out there will find this book, read it, and find help in it. Maybe they will read it and know that they are not alone in having a "broken brain."

That's the thing, my brain is broken. It isn't normal.

Was I born like this? Or did events in my life make me this way?

It's hard to say, even doctors aren't one hundred percent on why this happens to people, but then again, the reason for it doesn't matter.

It's dealing with it, coping with it that matters.

I still struggle with it weekly, sometimes daily, but I'm getting through it.

There are days that I wake up, and just want to go back to sleep and never wake up. That's honestly the hardest part of my day: waking up.

I know that throughout the first part of this book I mentioned I was lazy, but I've realized that it isn't just being lazy, it's not having the energy to do anything.

That's the thing with depression and anxiety, it leaves you drained, both physically and mentally. It makes it hard to do anything, even simple things like bathing and self-care, or even grocery shopping.

Yet, I still find a way to do it.

Most days.

It's been nearly four years since I wrote Part One.

A lot has happened in that time.

I've moved on from MJ, it took nearly two of those four years, but it happened. I went on dates, I hooked up with several women, and I had two more girlfriends.

The most recent relationship ending only a month ago.

I started school a month after I finished part one of this book, working towards a Bachelors in Game Art, it didn't take me long to realize that I was in the wrong field. I am now less than two months away from my Bachelors in Creative Writing. After that I'm going after my Masters.

I haven't worked since 2016, in fact I haven't done much with my life in the past four years.

Other than work on school, I've worked on healing.

Maybe I actually have done a lot?

Healing was hard. It took two counselors/therapists to help me through it. A dozen different medications. A new diagnosis of my "mental illnesses." Sleepless days and nights. Moving. Thoughts of suicide, but no attempts.

It took a lot of help to get here, to be where I am mentally, to be "steady."

I still have my off days, my down days, but I'm still alive. And the help I received, and still receive from friends and family, is truly what has gotten me through it.

I have done this, I have made it this far, with help, and on my own.

The one thing that I have learned from all of this is that you can get help from those around you, but you are the one that has to make the changes necessary to better your life, and yourself.

It also helps to be properly diagnosed.

Officially, I have Major Depressive Disorder, Generalized Anxiety Disorder, and a mix of Insomnia and Hypersomnia.

Ain't life grand?

I have fully realized that my mental disorders make up a lot of who I am, but they are not who I actually am. I know that they will always be a part of me, but I also know that they are something that I don't have to let control me.

I have to be the one to take control of my life.

I have to be the one in control.

Prologue

There are moments in your life where you seem like you are at the end of your rope, like everything around you is crashing down. That you have nothing to live for. That you have no purpose. That you have no choice but to end it all. That your only choice is to commit suicide.

Bullshit. Bull-fucking-shit.

I'm a hypocrite, I know. If you've reading this, then you know somewhat of my backstory, of my history. Of my three attempts at suicide. So, what the fuck do I know?

Where do I get off telling you that your suicidal thoughts are bullshit?

Who the fuck do I think I am?

I'll tell you. A survivor.

After three attempts at my life, I've realized that I'm a survivor.

Not of suicide, but of my brain.

If you are reading this, either as someone who suffers from a mental illness like Major Depressive Disorder or Bipolar Disorder, or as someone who struggles to see someone suffer with a mental illness, you have to know that you are not alone in any of this.

You. Are. Not. Alone.

I'm not a doctor. I'm not a psychiatrist. I'm not a therapist.

I'm just a twenty-eight-year-old-man, who has seen and experienced his fair share of life.

I'm not going to sit here and tell you what to do, you probably already have enough people in your life doing that already. But what I am going to do is continue to tell you my story.

About my struggles.

Maybe they can help you. Then again maybe you will think this is all bullshit.

Either way, I hope that you can take something away from reading this.

Hopefully, you can gain some perspective, even if it's nothing more than, "Jeez, this guy is a terrible writer, who is crazier than a wet sack full of kittens."

Remember the moment
You know exactly where you're goin'
'Cause the next moment before you know it
Time is slowin' and it's rolling still
And the windowsill looks really nice, right?
You think twice about your life
It probably happens at night, right?
Fight it, take the pain, ignite it
Tie a noose around your mind
Loose enough to breath fine and tie it
To a tree tell it, you belong to me, this ain't a
noose
This is a leash and I have news for you

You must obey me

Excerpt from *Holding on to You* – Twenty One Pilots

Chapter I

Pause

There are two outcomes to suicide:

You failed, you're alive.

You succeeded, you're dead.

Yet, that isn't true, at least not for those that survive you. If you succeed, you leave hurt behind for those around you. You leave an empty space in the hearts and souls of those who love you, and it's a void that can never be filled. Your pain may end, but theirs will just begin, and it will be an everlasting pain.

I survived my three attempts, I don't know how, but I did. I don't believe in god or religion. I'm not an atheist, at best you could call me an agnostic, but even then, that wouldn't be completely accurate.

I look back at my life and I see a lot of hurt, a lot of scars, some of the hurt and scars are my own, the rest I have caused for others.

Yet, I have to remember that my life continued, I moved on. I was hurt, I healed, and life continued.

I still think about my life, about the things that I have done, but I don't let them hurt me anymore. These moments may have left scars, but I'm still alive. And even though I still struggle with depression and suicidal thoughts, I still take those moments to pause and reflect on my past and my potential future. My mother always told me that "suicide is a permanent solution to a temporary problem."

Mother knows best.

Had I succeeded at any one of my attempts, I wouldn't be here writing to you now. I wouldn't be here sharing my story. My story isn't over, and even after I finish writing the second part of this book, I still have a long way to go. I just have to remember to pause. I just have to remember to take a step back, breath, and know that I have a choice in what happens in my life.

That same choice that you have.

"A semicolon is used when an author could've chosen to end their sentence, but chose not to. The author is you and the sentence is your life."

-Project Semicolon

Do you end your sentence? Or do you pause, take a breath, and continue living?

That choice is yours and only yours to make.

But remember who and what you leave behind.

I know just how hard the struggle can be, how daunting it can be to wake up every day and hurt just as much as the day before. Sometimes the struggle seems like it isn't worth it.

Like the juice isn't worth the squeeze.

But, I promise you, it is.

There is so much life to live. So much to do, so much to see, and it's all out there if you take the time to see it.

The things, the people that gets me through the day are my family and friends, especially my nieces and nephews. When things get so difficult, so hard that I don't want to be here anymore, I just remember that I still have to see them grow up. I'm their Uncle Kris, and I can't leave them behind. I want to watch them grow up. I want to sit on the front porch with a shotgun on prom night to scare their prom date. I want to see them graduate high school. I want to see them live their lives.

Even when my own life seems like it isn't worth living, their lives are worth living for.

No matter how hard things get, no matter how many suicidal thoughts I have, no matter how many plans I make to commit suicide, I have to remember to pause.

Because there is so much more for me to write about.

Chapter II

Ignorance is Bliss

I'm still not sure what the point is of part two, but here I am still writing it.

Maybe it's to show that life still moves forward.

With or without you.

When I found the file for part one, I reread it, and it made me realize just how crazy I sounded. I was obsessed with a girl who wanted nothing to do with me. I was obsessed with a relationship that was unhealthy and hostile, and by doing so I myself become unhealthy and hostile.

When I tried committing suicide that last time, I thought it was because of her.

I thought it was the fear of being alone without her.

Yes, being alone is hard, but it's something that everyone goes through on and off throughout their lives. It's miserable at best, yet, it's an opportunity to grow.

The thing you have to realize about being single, about being alone, is that it is truly an opportunity for growth. It's an opportunity to find who you are inside. I know, I know, it sounds cliché, but it's completely true.

It's a time for self-reflection. It's a time for self-realization.

And being with MJ I had lost myself. I forgot who I was. I forgot how to be happy with who I am. And that's the thing, you have to learn to be happy with yourself before you can ever truly be happy in a relationship.

I was so focused on making her happy, on helping her with her problems, on "fixing" her, that I completely ignored and forgot about my own. I ended up in the hospital broken, met her, and never fixed myself. Which is exactly the reason I ended up back in the hospital after we broke up.

I never got better.

When you struggle with depression, with anxiety, with suicidal thoughts and tendencies, you always try to find something to distract yourself from it, but that isn't healthy. Focusing on someone or something else so completely may feel good, because you aren't focusing on your pain, but it doesn't mean that it isn't there.

It is.

And when you don't take care of an open wound, it gets infected. It festers, it spreads.

It gets worse.

You can ignore your problems all you want, but they will still be there watching from the darkness.

Watching. Waiting.

And when you least expect it, it will rear its ugly head, only this time it may be too much for you to handle. That darkness inside you, that hurt, that pain, it can come back and bite you in the ass.

It doesn't matter how much money you have in the bank, how successful you are in life, how many people you have slept with, how "happy" you may feel. If you ignore the problems you have, they'll still be there.

You have to take care of yourself, of your brain first and foremost, otherwise nothing will get better.

I'm not going to lie to you and say that it's easy, it isn't. It's hard. It's really fucking hard, but you have to do it. You have to face that you have a problem. You have to find a way to fix it. You have to find a way to get better.

I've said it before, and I'll say it again.

The only person who can start to fix it, is you.

And I'll say it again.

You don't have to do it alone.

There are so many resources out there, so many people that you can call and talk to. You have friends and family you can depend on, even if you think you don't. I guarantee that there is at least one person you can confide in.

I guarantee it.

You. Are. Not. Alone. In. This.

Sorry if this comes off as preachy, I don't mean it to be.

It doesn't make it any less true though.

I mentioned earlier that it took me two years to get over MJ. Two fucking years.

Why?

Because I ignored my problems. Again, I know, I'm a hypocrite. I keep telling you to do the exact opposite of what I have done myself. And to be honest with you, I will probably continue to do so.

Do as I say, not as I do.

For two years I wallowed in self-pity. I didn't look for help. I didn't ask for help. I didn't want help. I just wanted to lay in bed, play video games, and cry myself to sleep.

This was the most productive I've ever been in my life.

That was sarcasm. Why isn't there a sarcasm font?

I was getting worse.

Every. Single. Day.

I was shriveling away. I was slowly dying inside. I gained weight, which is odd considering I rarely ate. I showered maybe once a week.

I was angry.

At the world. At my friends. At my family. At myself.

I had panic attacks almost daily. Sometimes to the point that I would lay frozen in bed, unable to speak, unable to breathe, unable to function. Hot tears streaming down my face.

I would scream so loud, yet there wasn't a single voice to be heard around me.

It was all inside. There were so many voices in my head, all yelling, all screaming, fighting to come to the surface. All of them saying different things. All of them me.

It was a war raging inside of my mind. A battle of darkness, of doubt, of pain, of suffering. And it was never ending.

And I was alone.

But, this was by choice. I didn't want to bother anyone with my thoughts, with my pain. It was mine to bear, not theirs. Why should I put any of it on them? They didn't deserve to hear my thoughts, they shouldn't be forced with the burden that is my brain, that is me.

I viewed myself as nothing more than a burden to those around me.

My world was nothing more than those screams inside my head. Those thoughts that would fight for control. It was as if my brain had so much noise in it, that the sounds all blurred together, forming nothing but static.

And it was loud.

It was the ringing in my ears, the thump, thump, thump of my heartbeat. Anything and everything could set me off. The world was too loud, so I locked myself in my room.

I locked myself in a cage, that only I had the key to.

Yet, I forgot I had the key the whole time.

It's like being in a prison of your own design. You are the prisoner, the guard, and the warden.

How did I break free?

I'm not sure exactly. I know that it wasn't any one thing, and I know that it wasn't easy.

Depression is never easy.

I'm not going to tell you the "one true fix" for depression, because there isn't one. And what worked for me, may not work for you. That you will have to figure out for yourself.

I can't tell you when things fit together in just the right way, or in what moment I knew that I was better. I can't tell you when I realized I needed to change.

What I can tell you is what worked for me, and how I got there.

There are so many aspects to being mentally healthy, some of which I am still working on, but there are two key factors of that are the most important for me.

Therapy and medication.

And like I said, what works for me, may not work for you.

It took a long time, years, and at least a dozen different medications to get me where I needed to be. The biggest problem with medication is finding ones without major side effects, that also help balance your mind and brain.

For me that balance was Cymbalta and Buspirone. Cymbalta for my depression, and Buspirone for my anxiety. I still suffer with insomnia, and no amount of medication has been able to fix that for me. And with insomnia comes hypersomnia, well, at least for me it does.

I still struggle with depression on a daily basis, but it's not as bad as it was. It's become manageable, and I think that is better than nothing. My baseline seems to be higher as well.

You may be wondering what I mean by "baseline."

By that I mean where my mood sits at regularly.

Let's say that a normal person has a baseline of zero, with zero being content, or at ease. You move positively, you get happier, you move negatively, you become sadder.

Make sense?

Well, for me four years ago, my baseline was easily a constant of negative six or seven. Now, with medication, I'm at a constant of negative two or three. It sucks, but it's still better. I've come to terms with not being at a zero, with being in a sort of constant state of depression, and I think because of that I've learned to cope better.

I realize that I will never truly be normal, that I will never be at a constant of zero. And I think that is another important step, self-realization, but we will come back to that later.

The other factor I mentioned is therapy.

Therapy is hard.

I used to say therapist like "the rapist," because I always felt like they raped your wallet, and then left you feeling numb, but things are different now.

I realized that you have to want to be better. That you have to go in with an honest and open mind.

Otherwise, what is the fucking point?

—

I've heard it said by a lot of different people that they hate going to the therapist. That they feel like nothing gets accomplished, that it's a waste of time, that they don't feel listened to. Blah, blah, blah.

I get it. It's already hard enough sharing how you really feel inside with someone you love, let alone a total stranger.

Especially when that stranger is writing shit down on a pad of paper.

It's also hard to trust someone you don't know, especially if you have had trust issues your whole life.

One thing I can tell you for sure is that for me I have a hard time opening up with the men in my life. I spent most of my childhood and adulthood with female friends.

I realized that a lot of my trust issues stem from my abusive stepfather, which is why therapy never seemed to work for me. Most of my therapists were men. It wasn't until I had my first female therapist that I really started to open up.

Did I come up with this on my own? No, of course not. My therapist helped me get there. She helped me to realize that I had these trust issues with others, and more so with men.

She also helped me to realize a lot about my relationship with MJ, but again, that'll come up later.

The point I'm trying to make is that therapy doesn't work if you aren't willing to make it work.

For me therapy helped me to realize so much about myself, so much that I needed to work on, so much that I needed to change.

Now we've come back full circle to what I mentioned earlier: self-realization.

I hate the term self-realization because it sounds like "self-help" mumbo jumbo, and to me self-help is filed right next to natural oils (aka snake oils).

There is a lot in this world that is bullshit, there are people out there that make a living off of misery, and sometimes it's hard to decipher what is real and what isn't. The only thing I can say about that is to trust your gut, to trust your instincts.

And you can trust them. Usually.

Sorry, I rambled again.

Where were we?

Self-realization.

To put it simply it is the realization of oneself. To see who you are inside, to truly see who you are inside, and not this image you put up for everyone else.

It's looking in the mirror and saying, "Hey, this is me, take it or leave it."

Once you say that, once you really see who you are, that's when you can start to make the changes you need to make. The changes for the better.

For me, I was seeing a child looking at me through a man's eyes.

I never grew up, I still haven't. I will always be a child at heart, and I don't think that will ever change, but it's realizing that my love of video games, farts, burps, and practical jokes doesn't have to get in the way of my life. It doesn't have to get in the way of my evolution into who I am meant to be.

I'm twenty-eight. I'm almost thirty. I'm a grown ass man who still lives at home. Yet, that isn't what I want out of life. I have dreams. I have goals. I have aspirations.

And I will never achieve them.

Not if I don't grow up.

Now that doesn't mean that I can't still be me. I can still play video games, I can still burp and fart, I can still make practical jokes.

But I have to be an adult.

I have to be an adult when it really matters.

If I really want to achieve anything in life, I have to get off my ass and work for it.

We don't deserve anything. We aren't entitled to anything.

If you want something, you have to put in the work, you have to earn it.

I see so many people my age that believe the world owes them something. It doesn't. And spending your life thinking that you are "owed" will just leave you with disappointment.

I have to grow up.

And so too do you.

Another of my "self-realizations" was that I have to start talking to people. I have to let them in.

If you live your life behind walls of your own design, you will never be happy.

And don't get me wrong, I'm not saying to let every single person in your life in, just a handful. You have to build a healthy support system. When you suffer from depression or bipolar disorder, or whatever, you have to have people you can count on.

I know this is hard, especially if you have lived your life being let down like I have, but it's something that you still need to do.

You have to know when to "sink or swim." You have to know when to let people in and when to let people go.

When your brain is already surrounded in darkness, do you really need more negativity in it? If you know someone isn't healthy for you, if a relationship isn't healthy for you, you have to know when to let go. It will probably hurt, but in the end, it will be for the best.

You have to surround yourself with people you can trust, with people you can talk to, and let go of the people that will abuse and hurt you.

Like for me, MJ.

But again, we will come back to that.

And it doesn't matter how much you have been through with that person, how much you may love them, if they are mistreating you, if they are bringing you down, you have to let go of them.

And just because someone is a blood relative, it doesn't mean they are family.

And I'm not saying that you have to "run" from your problems by letting go of people. That's not what I'm saying at all. I'm not telling you to run, I'm telling you to let go. Because some problems are only problems if you allow them to be.

I could sit here and tell you everything that I realized about myself, but that isn't the point of this chapter. The point of this chapter is to show things that helped me, so that you might find solutions for yourself. For me it was therapy and medication, it was tearing down walls that I had built around me and letting people in, it was looking inside at who I was versus who I wanted to be and making the necessary changes.

Like I've said though, what works for me may not work for you.

Regardless, if you are hurting, if you are in pain, get help. Please get help. Don't wait until it is too late. Don't wait until the blade is in your arm, the pills are in your stomach, or your car is smoking and smooshed and you are struggling to find your cigarettes.

Don't wait to be like me.

Don't ignore what is hurting you.

Find a way to fix it, to make it better.

Because suicide cannot be an option.

It is not an option.

Ever.

Chapter III

Portraits

I told you we would talk about MJ, and you know I keep my promises.

The hardest part of getting better, was letting go of MJ. I was pining for someone who was gone, for someone who wasn't real in the first place.

In Part One, I painted a picture of a girl who was flawed, but perfect for me.

That painting couldn't be further from the truth.

The thing is, I was still so hurt by the situation, by her, that I was blindly grasping at what I knew. I was looking for a girl who may have not been real, but instead a version of her that I created in my mind.

That is what happens when you are in love. You create an image in your head of the person you are with. A lot of time this person isn't actually them at all. You ignore their faults and glorify their "strengths." You only want to see the good in them.

Yet, what if that good wasn't there to begin with?

People always say that their exes are crazy, that they are evil, that they are this that or whatever, but if you really look back at them, are they really as bad as you think they are?

Generally, not. Usually you say these things to get over the hurt that you experienced with losing them.

But, occasionally, this "bad version" of the person you are talking about may actually be pretty spot on.

With most of my exes this isn't true at all, but with MJ it is. It really is.

But, I'm not going to write a chapter of me bad mouthing her. There isn't any point in that.

What this chapter is about is seeing her for who she really was, versus who I believed her to be, because I want you to be able to do the same with the people in your life.

I want you to really see them, and not the paintings of them.

Our relationship wasn't healthy, not in the slightest. We were codependent, jealous, vindictive, and downright mean. We brought out the worst in each other, or at least she brought at the worst in me.

I can't tell you who she is now, but I can tell you who she was then.

She was controlling, manipulative, and a compulsive liar. She made me into someone that I hated, and it took years to get back to who I was.

I based every relationship after her on her, and nobody seemed to live up to her standards. To the standards that I created in my mind, the standards that she helped put there.

Being in that kind of relationship gives you a warped world view. It twists and distorts everything you know to be true.

Yet, it makes you wonder how you get to that point of view in the first place. Is it something that you come up with on your own, or is it something that they help shape?

Personally, I think that you tend to adopt your significant others thinking. You become more like them, and they become more like you, but what if they stay the same? What if you are the only one that changes? What if they are manipulating you, training you, to see things the way they do?

In Part One, I blamed myself for everything that happened. It was my fault, I did it, she did nothing, she was an angel.

Yeah, that's bullshit.

I know I'm not innocent in what happened. I know that I could have done things differently.

But I also know that things weren't as simple as I made them out to be.

The fact is this: she cheated on me, she left me for another man, and then blamed me for her actions.

No, she didn't sleep with him until after we broke up, but sex isn't the only way to cheat. You can emotionally cheat on someone.

And that is exactly what she did, even if she would never admit it.

She messaged me on Facebook back in 2015.

"Are you ready to forgive me?"

My response was, "Forgive you for what?"

Her: "Hurting you."

Me: "It was so much more than that. You destroyed me. It wasn't just my heart that you broke that day. It was my spirit, my soul, it was every part of me. You were my best friend, my soul mate, my everything and you walked away and never looked back."

Me: "To answer your question"

Me: "Yes. I forgave you a long time ago.

Her: "Okay"

Me: "Why?"

Her: "I just don't want to go through living with that on my back."

Me: "If that's your way of apologizing, then yeah, I forgive you. I've got better things to do in my life then to hold a grudge. To be honest with you, you leaving me was the best thing that could have happened to me. It woke me up, it made me realize my potential, it made me realize I am meant for greater things in my life. I miss your family, I miss Molly (her dog) and I miss the girl I fell in love with nearly 5 years ago, but I have moved on. I'm better than I have ever been. I hope you are well and give molly a hug and a kiss for me."

She didn't respond to that.

"I just don't want to go through living with that on my back."

That's the kind of person that she was. She didn't care that she hurt me, she didn't care that she put me through pain, she only cared about herself. And that basically sums up the relationship.
We would talk off and on after that. I would send her messages or "novels" being angry or telling her I missed her, or whatever. I don't know what I was looking for. Closure maybe?
Then in August of 2016 we talked for the last time.
I had asked to talk to her one last time, but on the phone. I was really wanting closure this time. I had been in counseling, it was helping, and I thought that taking to her might help. I messaged her telling this in late July 2016.

Her: (phone number)

Me: "When should I call you? I don't know what your schedule is like."

I didn't hear from her for almost a month after this. Skip forward to mid-August.

Her: "Everything is crazy right now and I'm about to make a big move to *redacted*"

Her: "Sorry I haven't called or texted you back."

Me: "It's okay, no worries. Honestly, I haven't felt the need to talk to you anymore. I've been going to counseling and it has been helping me to realize a lot of things. I've come to terms with everything and I've forgiven you for everything that happened."

Her: "I didn't ever feel like I needed to be forgiven for anything to be completely honest with you. I didn't and I still don't see what I did wrong. I completely told you how I felt about things and yet I feel like you were mistaken by every word I said to you. It's not simple, but it's not too complex to figure out what went wrong."

Me: "It doesn't matter anymore. If you don't know what you did wrong and you feel that you didn't do anything wrong, then it shouldn't matter to you anyways. It doesn't matter to me either way. Just know that I look fondly on the time we had together, no matter how it ended."

Her: "okay"

We haven't spoken since.

I'm not going to lie to you and say that I didn't say or do anything wrong after we broke up. In fact, I went more than a little crazy. I messaged her constantly in the beginning. I would flip flop from being angry to missing her. At one point she even threatened me with a restraining order.

After that I stopped contact for a while. I would go months without saying anything. I would block her on Facebook, and then unblock her a few months later and message her, just to block her again.

I was obsessed. I didn't know how to let go. It was unhealthy, and it was wrong.

And counselling/therapy helped me to see that.

But, the whole reason I even put those messages in here is to show you the amount of indifference that she had towards me. She didn't care.

She had moved on.

And that is what hurt me the most.

Like I said, this chapter isn't about me bad mouthing her, and I know that it may seem that way, but I'm not. I'm trying to prove a point.

She had moved on.

I hadn't.

I wasn't able to for a long time. And I hated her for it.

Yes, she hurt me. Yet, I was the one who continued to hurt myself by not letting go.

These messages may look like I'm trying to paint her in some evil light, but I'm trying to show how my mind worked at the time.

I really thought that about her. I really thought that she was the spawn of Satan. I referred to her as she-devil anytime she was brought up in conversation.

I had created this portrait of her in my mind. One of a monster, when in fact I had become the monster.

Yet, was I wrong? Was she a monster? I still struggle with that concept, and you have probably noticed that just in this chapter alone.

I keep flip flopping on how I feel about this even as I write it.

Was she the monster I believed her to be? Or was this just another portrait that I created?

It's hard to say. Maybe a bit of both?

I think it's all based upon perspective.

They say that memories are actually you remembering the last time you remembered something. If that's the case, can our minds change our perspective on our past? Can our perspective change purely on our current situation in life?

I don't hate MJ, I hate what happened, I hate what I became after it ended, but I don't hate her. And you shouldn't hate her either. She was living her life the way she was meant to live it, just like I was and am now.

People will come and go in your life, and there really isn't anything that you can do about it. You can either learn to let go, or you can hold on to the ever-changing memories and live your life in misery.

Chapter IV
Barbara

I feel as though my most recent ex should have her own chapter, because quite honestly, she was an important part of my healing process, but we will get to that in a second.

Every relationship I have been in has been with someone who has a lot of baggage. Someone who has a lot of issues that aren't healthy. I don't know if that is what I look for in another person, or if I just attract people like that.

Like attracts like, right?

Barbara, what a sweet girl.

We had our problems, but I loved her intently. I still love her, but I know that we didn't work. Just like there is a part of me that still loves MJ. Just like there is a part of me that still loves all of my exes. That's the thing, there will always be a part of you that still loves that person you used to be with for one reason or another. That love doesn't just go away. It may fade, it may crumble, but it never dies. The flame will always be there in one way or another.

Barbara was essentially the person that got me out of my funk, that got me out of my prison cell. She saw through that storm cloud that I had become. She was the sunlight that came through the darkness. And she made me see me for who I really was. That's just how she is.

Like I mentioned earlier, I haven't worked since 2016, yet she didn't care. She took care of me. She took me on dates, on "bookventures" (we'd go to used book stores and buy a bunch of books), to the movies, to dinner. It was the first relationship that I felt like I was being taken care of, and not the other way around.

I think that this was something that I needed. She was what I needed.

Yet, I've realized that she was what I needed, in the moment.

That's why it didn't work I think. I loved her, I cared about her, but at the end of the day, we just weren't compatible. We wanted different things from life. We were moving in different directions, and neither of us wanted to change that for each other.

We were together for over a year, and it was a rocky year, but that isn't why she gets her own chapter. If I wanted to write a book about all of my exes, I could, but I'd rather not.

Her chapter is about how she helped push me in the direction that I needed to be. She set forth the change in my life. She helped me see who I wanted to be, how to get there, and that I was capable and deserving of love.

Just as she made me see me for me, she too saw me for me, and she still loved me. She didn't run, she didn't try to change me. Instead she tried to lift me up, to make me stronger, and that's exactly what she did.

For that I will be eternally grateful.

Yet, I don't think that is what this chapter is about either.

I think that this chapter is to show that people will come and go in your life, and they can help you change. They can help you grow.

The change may not always be good, just as it may not be bad, but they will still spark that change. The thing is, you have to let them in. Some people may fight tooth and nail to get to you, while others may give up, and move on.

The ones that fight to get to you, are the ones that you should keep around.

I say should because it doesn't always work out that way.

The thing you have to understand about me is that I love passionately, violently. It may take me a while to get there, but once I do, you have all of me. It's because of this that breakups are so hard for me.

I've never stayed friends with an ex, no matter how much I may have wanted to keep them in my life, no matter how hard I tried to keep them a part of me. It just doesn't work. It may seem selfish of me, but it's just how my brain works.

And with Barbara it wasn't any different.

We broke up twice in single week. The first time for a few hours, the second for good. We broke up mutually, and cordially. We tried not contacting one another for a week, but we didn't make it that far. And in the end, we cried and yelled at each other, we were hurting. We decided once again to not talk for a week. We still wanted to be a part of each other's lives, but we also needed time to heal.

The radio silence didn't last very long. I made first contact, but she told me that she almost did several times. We were both weak. We loved each other, we wanted to be together, yet we both knew we couldn't.

That's the hardest part about being an adult, breaking up. We are supposed to be adults in this kind of situation, to be calm, to be respectful, but it usually never happens that way.

And this time was no different. And like that she was gone.

—

It's only been about a month, but I haven't reached out to her, and neither has she to me.

I have hated it, but at the same time, I know it's for the best. And if there is one thing I learned from MJ, it's that you have to know when to let go.

So, I have.

Even though it hurt, and still hurts now and then, I am still grateful to Barbara for the time that we had together. I am grateful for the changes that she sparked within me.

Changes that are still in the process of forming.

Thank you, Barbara.

Chapter V

The End – For Real This Time

I wrote part one in one sitting. The beginning all the way to chapter Sixteen, everything else was just a manic episode.

To be honest with you Part Two may just be another manic episode.

I'm not sure if the doctors have it right this time around. They say I have Major Depressive Disorder, yet they originally said that I have Bipolar Disorder.

It honestly might be a bit of both.

The reason I mention this is that the doctors may not always get everything right. When it comes to the human brain we still have a lot to learn.

And I think that applies to life in general.

We're born, we live, we die.

What's the point?

What is our purpose?

I know that everyone asks these questions.

I know that I do.

I'm not going to say that I know the answer to those questions, but I will say that I know it's a learning experience.

We live and we learn.

Yet, we seem to make the same mistakes over and over. We give advice that we don't follow ourselves.

Why do we do this? Why do we see the problems of others so easily, yet completely ignore our own problems?

If we just focused on our problems and didn't let the outside noise get in the way, our lives could be so much easier!

Easier said than done.

It isn't easy learning from past mistakes, not because we aren't willing to learn, but instead because we are unwilling to change.

Change is hard.

I went to a chiropractor a few months ago, and he said that we grow accustomed to pain. That our bodies get used to it and learn to live with it. That we adapt to deal with it.

We grow accustomed to pain. We adapt to deal with it.

Why do we do this? Why do we allow ourselves to stay in pain, instead of finding and fixing the problem?

It's okay to be prepared to be hurt, or even expect it, but it isn't okay to live life in constant pain.

So why do we do it?

Change. Is. Hard.

The question is, does it have to be?

Evolution is a reality. We've seen it in human history, we've seen it in the wild.

We create. We adapt. We learn.

If we are able to grow and adapt as a species, why can't we do it as individuals?

We have to stop being so scared to change, to evolve as a person.

We have to stop being so scared to get hurt.

Being hurt is inevitable, so why run from it. Just because something can happen doesn't mean that it actually will.

Murphy's Law is a lie.

I could walk outside right this second and get hit by a meteor, yet, it doesn't keep me from going outside.

So, why should I hide myself from the world, from people, just because I might get hurt?

If we live like this we will all die alone. I mean in the grand scheme of things we all eventually do die alone, but that's neither here nor there.

You know what I mean.

I guess all I am trying to say is don't fear change, embrace it, allow it to happen. Look for ways to better your life. Find things that make you happy, that bring your baseline to zero, because living in the negative sucks ass.

I know this first hand.

And you may be asking me, "what do I need to change?"

I don't fucking know, you have to find out for yourself.

It's like I've said from the beginning, you have to be the change you want to see in the world.

Wait, no, Gandhi said that. Well, at least something along those lines.

You get the idea.

You have to be the one to do it. You have to be the one to live your life, and you have to be the one who makes the hard decisions. You can't let anyone else do it for you. Not your parents, not your friends, not your family, not me.

Especially not me.

That's a terrible idea.

Chapter VI

Okay, I Lied.

Chapter Five really was supposed to be the last chapter. It really was.

Yet, here we are.

I can't seem to make up my mind.

Have you noticed the trend?

I've struggled to figure out what the point of my story is, of why I am telling it to you. I've struggled to find an answer.

I finally realized that there isn't a point to it, just as there isn't a point to anything that happens. We aren't "destined" for greatness. We aren't able to do anything and everything that we set our minds to.

Our teachers, our parents, they all lied to us.

And like suckers we bought into it.

We are our generations Shake Weight.

Yet, at the same time, maybe they didn't lie to us.

Maybe we just misunderstood them.

After being told our whole lives that our dreams, our hopes, our desires, our aspirations, whatever we wanted was attainable, and then coming to find out that they weren't...

It was heartbreaking.

Yet, were we actually lied to?

The more I think about it, the more I realize they never lied to us, not once. Well, at least not about this.

We just heard them wrong. It was all a big misunderstanding.

What they said was, "You can be whatever you want to be. You can have whatever you want in life."

What we heard was, "You can be whatever you want to be. You can have whatever you want in life. And it will all be given to you free of charge."

I mentioned in Chapter Two that we aren't entitled to anything. And I still believe in this, yet at the same time I think that we are entitled to everything the world has to offer.

But, we have to earn it.

And I think that is the point of all of this.

Of all of my rambling.

In telling my story.

It's that I earned the right to tell it.

How?

By staying alive.

I failed at suicide three times. I have the scars to prove it. I have the memories, I have the knowledge, and I'm going to use them all to my advantage.

I'm going to make the world my bitch. You should too.

You are given one life to live.

Don't you dare fucking waste it.

Epilogue

I just want to say thank you. I know this has been a rollercoaster of a read but thank you for sticking with me to the end. I hope you can take away something from this and learn from it just as I have from writing it. This story may be over, but my story isn't over, far from it, but this is what I wanted to share.

Thank you for letting me share it with you.

-Kristofer

P.S

Always wear your fucking seat belt.

You are not alone.

If you are struggling with suicide or know someone who is, please reach out. There are so many different avenues you can take, so many people that can help you. I know it is hard, but don't give up.

Please, get some help.

National Suicide Prevention Lifeline: 1-800-273-TALK (8255)

You can also text the crisis line, text "START" to 741-741

SuicidePreventionLifeline.org

Suicide Hotline: 1-800-SUICIDE (784-2433)

Ibpf.org

ProjectSemicolon.com

About the Author

Kristofer West is a novelist, short story author, poet, and avid gamer. He has an undying passion for Star Wars and Wookiees (some might even say obsession). He is currently writing a Science Fiction and Fantasy novel, written with the idea that all legends and myths are based upon factual events. The novel is expected to be finished some time before he dies of old age, eventually leading to a trilogy.

You can see his short stories at his blog:

http://fuzzieewookiee.blogspot.com